This Picture Gospel was Presented

To ....

By ....

On .... 20 ....

Jesus answered,

"I am the way and the truth and the life.

No one comes to the Father except through me.

John 14:6

JEBS

Picture Gospel in 40 Days

영어로 그림전도

[영어로 그림전도]의 원리와 학습방법

이 프로그램은 복음의 원리를 영어로 쉽게 설명할 수 있도록 만들어진 획기적인 전도 및 영어학습 프로그램이다.

"복음을 영어로 설명할 수 있도록 공부한다"고 하면 굉장히 어려울 것 같지만 정철 선생이 새로 개발한 A.D. 영어학습법을 따라 하면 아주 쉽게 익힐 수 있다.

이 새로운 학습법은 정철 선생이 오랫동안 기도와 실험 끝에 터득한 새로운 영어학습 개념이다. 지금까지 10년 넘게 공부를 해도, 고생만 하고 영어는 안되는 옛날식 B.C. 학습법 (Before Christ)을 버리고, 정철 선생이 주님께 받은 새로운 A.D. 학습법 (Anno Domini)으로 공부한다.

A.D. 영어학습법에 관한 상세한 얘기는 2023년 6월에 출간된 "정철의 A.D. 영어학습법"을 꼭 읽어 보시기 바란다.
본격적으로 이 프로그램을 공부하기 전에 우선 급한대로 A.D. 학습법의 요체를 몇 가지 설명하면,

1 영어는 낱개 단어로 움직이는 것이 아니라, 의미 단위로 몇 개씩 단어들이 모여서 움직인다. 이 묶음 단위를 '청크'라고 부른다. 영어의 청크는 6가지가 있다.

2 단어 묶음 '청크'들은 궁금한 순서로 나열된다. 영어 문장을 볼 때는 이 궁금한 순서를 느끼면서 이해하면 되고, 말을 할 때도 그 순서로 말한다.

따로 문법을 따질 필요가 없다.

3 이 청크들은 영어의 독특한 억양, 강세와 리듬으로 박자 맞춰 흘러간다.

4 이 문장들은 그냥 억지로 외우면 안 되고, 원어민의 소리와 똑같이 따라하면서 반복 낭송하다 보면 저절로 익혀진다.

5 좋은 문장들을 이렇게 반복 낭송하면 바위에 글씨가 새겨지듯이 머릿속에 깊이 새겨지게 된다. 이렇게 저절로 암송되는 문장들이 축적되어서 임계량에 이르게 되면 자연스럽게 영어가 열리게 된다.

6 본 교재를 보면, 마치 만화책처럼 그림들이 있고, 그림 단위별로 영어 문장들이 쓰여 있는 것을 볼 수가 있다. 이 그림들은 보통 어린이 동화책에 있는 삽화들과는 아주 다른 것이다. 정철 선생이 창안하여 발명특허를 획득한 [삽화 기억술]에 의한 그림들이다. 그림을 따라가면서 청크 단위로 말을 하다보면 어느새 전체 문장들을 자연스럽게 말하게 된다.

선교지에서 이 그림들을 보여주면서 영어로 설명을 하면 복음을 더 쉽고 선명하게 전할 수 있다.

[English Picture Gospel]
Key Ideas and Learning Approach

This program is a unique tool for learning English and evangelism. It simplifies explaining the gospel in English. If you follow the A.D. English learning method developed by Teacher Jungchul, it's quite easy. This method, created after much prayer and experimentation, moves away from traditional and less effective techniques.

For more on the A.D. English learning method, check out "Jungchul's A.D. English Learning Method," published in June 2023.

Here's a quick look at the A.D. English learning method:

1. English moves in chunks of meanings, not just single words.

2. Chunks follow a specific order that makes sense when you feel it in sentences.

3. English's unique rhythm comes from these chunks.

4. Mimicking native speakers and repeating good sentences help learn them naturally.

5. Repetitive practice deeply embeds these sentences in your memory, eventually making English flow naturally.

6. The program uses special illustrations, like in a comic book, to make learning engaging. These are not just any drawings but are designed using a patented technique by Teacher Jungchul. Talking through these pictures helps you naturally form complete English sentences.

This method is especially effective in missions, making it easier to communicate the gospel clearly.

교재의 구성

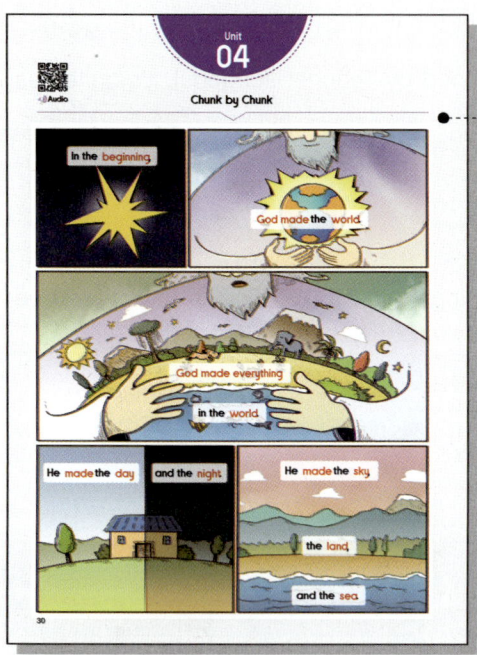

Chunk by Chunk

Understand the text in chunks.

그림을 보면서 청크 단위로 이해한다.

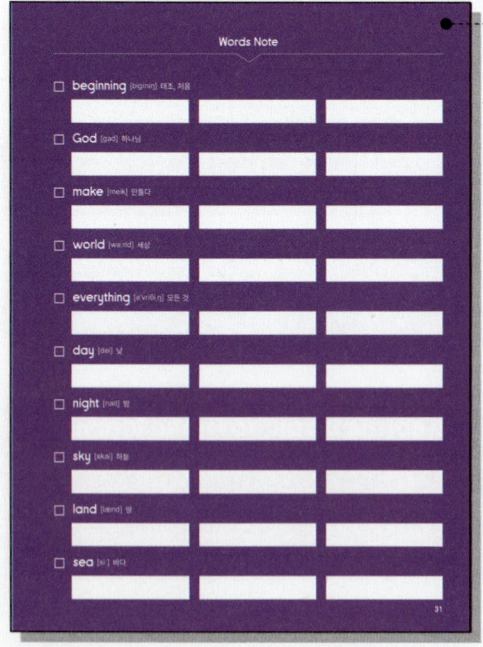

Words Note

Study the key words related to the text. They are presented with a pronunciation key and definition.

주요 단어들의 뜻을 익힌다.

Trace and Write

Trace and write the text in chunks.

우리말을 보며 궁금한 순서대로 흘러가는 어순 감각을 느끼면서 영어 문장을 베껴 쓴다.

Caption

Review the text by completing the caption writing activity.

그림을 보면서 영어 문장 캡션을 완성한다.

Pocket Book

Preach the gospel using the whole text you recited through the Illustrative Mnemonic Technique.

그림을 보며 삽화기억술로 암송한 내용으로 복음을 전도한다.

삽화기억술로 영어로 그림전도를 학습하는 방법

본 교재는 삽화기억술이 적용되어 있습니다. 완성도 높은 학습을 위해서 온라인 강의를 반드시 시청하기를 권장해 드립니다.

 본 온라인 강의는 '젭스' ▶ YouTube 채널 (youtube.com/@JEBS.OFFICIAL) 에서 시청할 수 있습니다.

Viewing
그림을 보며 배울 내용을 유추해보기

Listening
먼저 그림만 보며 원어민 음원을 듣고 따라하기

Pointing
삽화기억술에 따라 각 청크에 해당하는 그림을 짚어가며 듣고 따라하기

Shadowing
배운 내용을 그림을 보며 원어민 음원과 동시에 따라하기

Storytelling
배운 내용을 그림만 보며 영어로 말해보기

TABLE OF CONTENTS

- [영어로 그림전도]의 원리와 학습방법   4
- 교재의 구성   6
- 삽화기억술로 영어로 그림전도를 학습하는 방법   8

P — Heaven or Hell?
- Unit 01   14
- Unit 02   18
- Unit 03   24

01 — Who made the world?
- Unit 04   30
- Unit 05   34

02 — Why did God make mankind?
- Unit 06   40

03 — What did they do wrong?
- Unit 07   48
- Unit 08   52

04 — What happened to Adam and Eve?
- Unit 09   60
- Unit 10   64

05 Why did God punish them?

Unit 11 — 72
Unit 12 — 78
Unit 13 — 82

06 Are we also sinners? And what will happen to sinners?

Unit 14 — 88
Unit 15 — 92

07 What is Hell like?

Unit 16 — 98
Unit 17 — 102
Unit 18 — 108

08 Then, what is Heaven like?

Unit 19 — 114
Unit 20 — 118
Unit 21 — 122

09 What do people do to go to Heaven instead of Hell?

Unit 22 — 128
Unit 23 — 134

10 Then, how could people be forgiven?

Unit 24 — 140
Unit 25 — 146

11 · What was God's plan?
Unit 26 — 154
Unit 27 — 158

12 · What happened to Jesus after that?
Unit 28 — 166
Unit 29 — 172

13 · Then, what should I do?
Unit 30 — 178
Unit 31 — 184
Unit 32 — 190

14 · The Salvation Prayer
Unit 33 — 198
Unit 34 — 204
Unit 35 — 208

15 · Then, what should I do from now on?
Unit 36 — 214
Unit 37 — 220
Unit 38 — 226

16 · Where should we go?
Unit 39 — 234
Unit 40 — 240

A
- The Lord's Prayer — 248
- The Apostles' Creed — 250

- Bible Note — 254

Preface

P

Heaven or Hell?

Unit 01

Chunk by Chunk

Audio

Everyone wants to live a happy life.

So, we make every possible effort.

However, whether we live well off or not,

we all die sooner or later.

And this is not the end.

Words Note

☐ **want** [want, wɔ:nt] ~하기를 원하다, ~하고 싶다

☐ **live** [liv] (동족 목적어와 함께) ~한 생활을 하다(보내다) *live a ... life

☐ **make** [meik] 하다, 행하다

☐ **possible** [pásəbl] 가능한

☐ **effort** [éfərt] 노력

☐ **however** [hauévər] 그러나, 그렇지만

☐ **well off** 부유한, 잘사는

☐ **die** [dai] 죽다

☐ **sooner or later** 조만간, 머잖아

☐ **end** [end] 끝

Trace and Write

천국입니까 아니면 지옥입니까

Heaven or Hell?

사람은 누구나 원합니다 / 행복한 삶을 살기를

Everyone wants / to live a happy life.

그래서 / 우리는 합니다 모든 가능한 노력을

So, / we make every possible effort.

하지만 / 우리가 잘 살건 아니건 /

However, / whether we live well off or not, /

우리는 모두 죽습니다 / 조만간

we all die / sooner or later.

그런데 / 이것이 끝이 아닙니다

And / this is not the end.

Caption

Unit 02

Chunk by Chunk

Words Note

- **die** [dai] 죽다

- **judge** [dʒʌdʒ] 심판하다

- **send** [send] ~에 보내다

- **either** [íːðər] [둘 중] 어느 쪽 하나

- **live** [liv] 살다

- **happily** [hǽpili] 행복하게

- **forever** [fəreˈvər] 영원히

- **sadness** [sǽdnis] 슬픔

- **pain** [pein] 고통

☐ **beautiful** [bjúːtəfəl] 아름다운

☐ **paradise** [pǽrədàis] 낙원

☐ **great** [greit] 큰, 거대한

☐ **horrible** [hɔ́ːrəbl, hɑ́rəbl] 무서운, 끔찍한

☐ **lake** [leik] 호수; 연못

Trace and Write

우리는 죽으면 /

When we die, /

___

우리는 심판을 받습니다 /

we are judged, /

___

그리고 보내집니다 천국이나 지옥 둘 중 하나로

and sent to either Heaven or Hell.

___

만약 우리가 천국으로 가면 /

If we go to Heaven, /

___

우리는 행복하게 삽니다 영원히 /

we live happily forever, /

슬픔 없이 / 그리고 고통 없이 /

with no sadness / and no pain, /

아름다운 낙원에서

in the beautiful paradise.

그러나 / 만약 우리가 지옥으로 가면 /

But, / if we go to Hell, /

우리는 큰 고통 속에서 삽니다 영원히 /

we live in great pain forever /

무서운 불못에서

in the horrible lake of fire.

Caption

Unit 03

Chunk by Chunk

Words Note

- **think** [θiŋk] 생각하다

- **take** [teik] (시간 등을) 내다

- **a few** … 몇 개의, 약간의 ~

- **minute** [mínit] (시간 단위의) 분

- **read** [ri:d] 읽다

- **find** [faind] 발견하다, 찾아내다

- **amazing** [əméiziŋ] 놀라운

- **truth** [tru:θ] 진리, 진실

- **change** [tʃeindʒ] 바꾸다, 변화시키다

- **life** [laif] 인생

Trace and Write

어디라고 당신은 생각합니까 / 당신이 갈 곳이 /

Where do you think / you will go, /

천국입니까 아니면 지옥입니까

Heaven or Hell?

그저 몇 분만 시간을 내서 /

Just take a few minutes /

이 소책자를 읽어 보세요

and read this booklet.

당신은 발견할 것입니다 그 놀라운 진리를 /

You will find the amazing truth /

당신의 인생을 바꾸게 될

that will change your life.

Caption

Chapter 01

Who made the world?

Unit 04

Chunk by Chunk

Words Note

☐ **beginning** [bigínin] 태초, 처음

☐ **God** [gad] 하나님

☐ **make** [meik] 만들다

☐ **world** [wə:rld] 세상

☐ **everything** [e'vriθi,ŋ] 모든 것

☐ **day** [dei] 낮

☐ **night** [nait] 밤

☐ **sky** [skai] 하늘

☐ **land** [lænd] 땅

☐ **sea** [si:] 바다

Trace and Write

누가 세상을 만들었을까요

Who made the world?

___

태초에 /

In the beginning, /

___

하나님이 세상을 만드셨습니다

God made the world.

___

하나님은 모든 것을 만드셨습니다 / 세상에

He made everything / in the world.

___

그분은 낮을 만드셨습니다 / 그리고 밤을

He made the day / and the night.

___

그분은 하늘을 만드셨습니다 / 땅을 / 그리고 바다를

He made the sky, / the land, / and the sea.

Caption

Unit 05

Chunk by Chunk

Words Note

- [ ] **make** [meik] 만들다

- [ ] **plant** [plænt] 식물

- [ ] **land** [lænd] 땅

- [ ] **moon** [muːn] 달

- [ ] **star** [staːr] 별

- [ ] **sky** [skai] 하늘

- [ ] **fish** [fiʃ] 물고기

- [ ] **sea** [siː] 바다

- [ ] **bird** [bəːrd] 새

- [ ] **animal** [ǽnəməl] 동물, 짐승

Trace and Write

그분은 식물들을 만드셨습니다 / 땅 위에

He made the plants / on the land.

그분은 해를 만드셨습니다 / 달을 /

He made the sun, / the moon, /

그리고 별들을 / 하늘에

and the stars / in the sky.

그러고 나서 / 그분은 물고기들을 만드셨습니다 / 바다에 /

Then, / He made the fish / in the sea, /

새들을 하늘에 /

the birds in the sky, /

그리고 동물들을 땅 위에

and the animals on the land.

Caption

Chapter 02

Why did God make mankind?

Unit 06

Chunk by Chunk

God made mankind —

a man and a woman.

Why did God make them?

To love and to be loved.

God loved them so much

that He blessed them.

Words Note

- [ ] **God** [gad] 하나님

- [ ] **make** [meik] 만들다

- [ ] **mankind** [mænkaínd] 인간, 인류

- [ ] **man** [mæn] 남자

- [ ] **woman** [wúmən] 여자

- [ ] **love** [lʌv] 사랑하다

- [ ] **much** [mʌtʃ] 많이

- [ ] **bless** [bles] 축복하다

Trace and Write

왜 하나님은 인간을 만드셨을까요

Why did God make mankind?
_____

하나님은 인간을 만드셨습니다 /

God made mankind — /
_____
_____
_____

한 남자와 한 여자로

a man and a woman.
_____
_____
_____

왜 / 하나님은 그들을 만드셨을까요

Why / did God make them?
_____
_____
_____

사랑하기 위해서 / 그리고 사랑 받기 위해서
To love / and to be loved.

하나님은 그들을 사랑하셨습니다 매우 많이 /
God loved them so much /

그래서 그분은 그들을 축복하셨습니다
that He blessed them.

Caption

Gospel Questions

1. Who made mankind?

2. Why did God make them?

Chapter
03

What did they do wrong?

 Audio

Chunk by Chunk

Words Note

- [ ] **do** [du, də; (강) duː] 하다

- [ ] **wrong** [rɔ́ːŋ] 잘못, 틀리게

- [ ] **say** [sei] 말하다

- [ ] **eat** [iːt] 먹다

- [ ] **any** [éni] 어느, 어떤

- [ ] **tree** [triː] 나무

- [ ] **knowledge** [nάlidʒ] 앎, 지식

- [ ] **good** [gud] 선(善)

- [ ] **evil** [íːvəl] 악, 사악

- [ ] **die** [dai] 죽다

Trace and Write

무엇을 그들은 했습니까 잘못되게

What did they do wrong?

하나님은 말씀하셨습니다 남자 아담에게 /

God said to the man — Adam,

너는 먹을 수 있다 / 어느 나무로부터든지

"You can eat / from any tree.

그러나 먹지 마라 /

But do not eat /

그 나무로부터 / 선과 악을 알게 하는

from the tree / of the knowledge of good and evil,

그렇지 않으면 너는 죽을 것이다

Or you will die."

Caption

Unit 08

Chunk by Chunk

Words Note

- **disguise** [disgáiz] 변장하다, 가장하다

- **snake** [sneik] 뱀

- **tempt** [tempt] 유혹하다

- **eat** [i:t] 먹다

- **fruit** [fru:t] 과일

- **like** [laik] ~처럼

- **finally** [fáinəli] 결국, 마침내

- **give** [giv] 주다

- **another** [ən ðər] 다른, 또 하나의

- **too** [tu:] ~도 또한

Trace and Write

어느 날 /

One day, /

사탄이 / 변장한 뱀으로 /

Satan, / disguised as a snake, /

유혹했습니다 여자 이브를

tempted the woman — Eve.

만약 네가 그 과일을 먹는다면 /

"If you eat the fruit, /

너는 될 것이다 하나님처럼

you will be like God."

결국 / 이브는 그 과일을 먹었습니다 /

Finally, / Eve ate the fruit /

그리고 다른 하나를 주었습니다 아담에게 /

and gave another to Adam, /

그리고 그는 그것을 먹었습니다 또한

and he ate it, too.

Caption

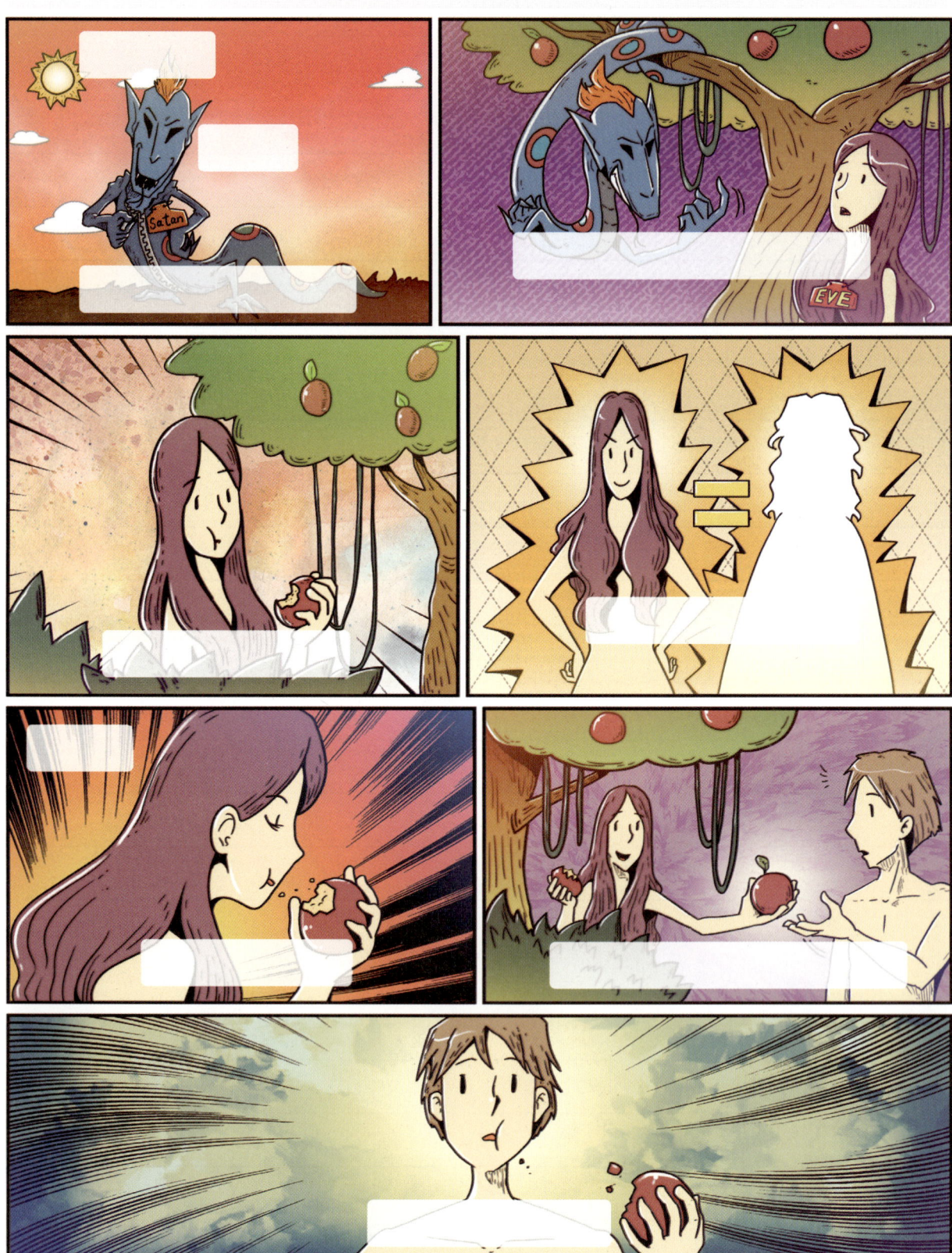

Gospel Questions

1. Who tempted Adam and Eve?

2. How did Satan tempt them to eat from the Tree of Knowledge?

Chapter 04

What happened to Adam and Eve?

Unit 09

Chunk by Chunk

Words Note

- **happen to** ... ~에게 일어나다

- **punish** [pʌniʃ] 처벌하다, 벌하다

- **say** [sei] 말하다

- **great** [greit] 큰, 많은

- **pain** [pein] 고통

- **have a baby** 아이를 낳다

- **husband** [hʌzbənd] 남편

- **rule over** ... ~을 지배하다

Trace and Write

무슨 일이 일어났나요 아담과 이브에게

What happened to Adam and Eve?

하나님은 그들을 벌하셨습니다

God punished them.

하나님은 말씀하셨습니다 이브에게 /

God said to Eve, /

너는 있게 될 것이다 큰 고통 속에 /

"You will be in great pain /

네가 아기를 낳을 때

when you have babies.

그리고 너의 남편이 지배할 것이다 너를

And your husband will rule over you."

Caption

Unit 10

Chunk by Chunk

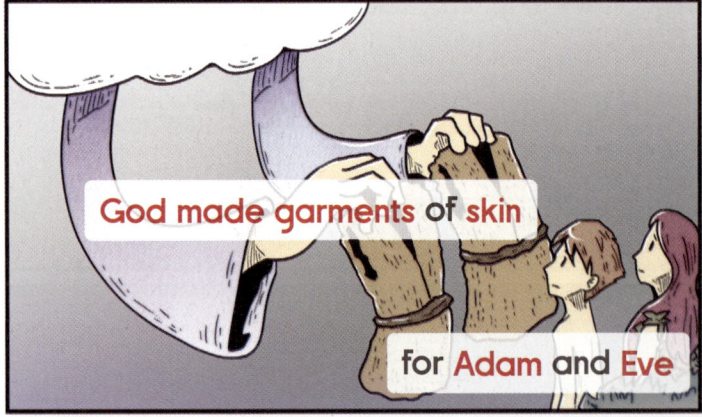

Words Note

- [ ] **say** [sei] 말하다

- [ ] **work** [wəːrk] 일하다

- [ ] **food** [fuːd] 음식

- [ ] **make ··· out of ···** ~에서 ~를 만들다

- [ ] **dust** [dʌst] 흙

- [ ] **return** [ritə́ːrn] (원래의 장소 등으로) (되)돌아가다

- [ ] **garment** [gáːrmənt] 옷, 의복

- [ ] **skin** [skin] 가죽

- [ ] **clothe** [klouð] (옷을) 입히다

- [ ] **drive ··· out of ···** ~에서 ~를 몰아내다, 내쫓다

Trace and Write

하나님은 말씀하셨습니다 아담에게 /

God said to Adam, /

너는 일을 해야 한다 음식을 위해

"You must work for food.

그리고 너는 만들어졌다 흙으로부터 /

And you were made out of dust, /

따라서 너는 돌아갈 것이다 그것으로

so you will return to it."

하나님은 만드셨습니다 가죽으로 된 옷을 /

God made garments of skin /

아담과 이브를 위해 /

for Adam and Eve /

그리고 그들을 입히셨습니다

and clothed them.

그리고는 그분은 그들을 내쫓으셨습니다 에덴 밖으로

And He drove them out of Eden.

Caption

Gospel Questions

1. Did God punish Adam?

2. What was the punishment for Adam?

Chapter 05

Why did God punish them?

Unit
11

Audio

Chunk by Chunk

Words Note

- **punish** [pʌniʃ] 처벌하다, 벌하다

- **severely** [sivíərli] 심하게, 격렬하게

- **just** [dʒʌst] 그저, 단지

- **eat** [i:t] 먹다

- **some** [səm; (강) sʌm] 몇

- **fruit** [fru:t] 과일

- **listen to** … ~을 듣다

- **follow** [fálou] 따르다

- **moment** [móumənt] 순간

- **enter into** … ~안으로 들어가다

Trace and Write

왜 / 하나님은 그들을 벌하셨을까요

Why / did God punish them?

왜 / 하나님은 그들을 벌하셨을까요 / 그토록 가혹하게 /

Why / did God punish them / so severely /

그들이 먹기만 했는데 과일 몇 개를

when they just ate some fruit?

그것은 ~때문입니다 / 그들이 하나님의 말씀을 듣지 않고 /

It's because / they didn't listen to God /

그들이 사탄을 따랐기 때문입니다

but they followed Satan.

그 순간에 / 그들이 사탄을 따랐던 /

The moment / they followed Satan. /

사탄은 들어갔습니다 그들 안으로

Satan entered into them.

Caption

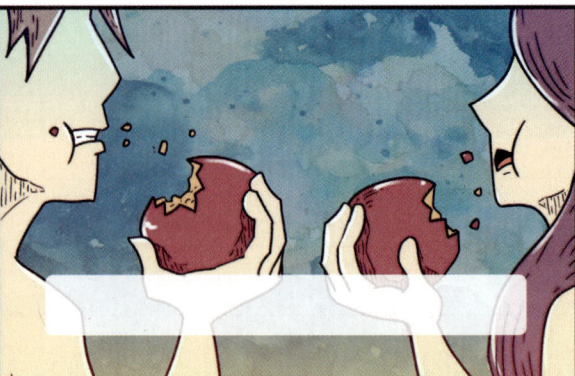

Gospel Questions

1. Why did God punish Adam and Eve?

2. What happened when they followed Satan?

Unit 12

Chunk by Chunk

Words Note

☐ **become** [bikʌm] ~이 되다

☐ **king** [kiŋ] 왕

☐ **slave** [sleiv] 노예

☐ **think** [θiŋk] 생각하다

☐ **act** [ækt] 행동하다

☐ **speak** [spi:k] 말하다

☐ **mind** [maind] 마음

☐ **call** [kɔ:l] [사람, 사물을] (어떤 이름으로) 부르다

☐ **sinful** [sínfəl] 죄가 되는, 죄악의

☐ **nature** [néitʃər] 본성

Trace and Write

사탄은 되었습니다 그들의 왕이 /

Satan became their king /

그리고 그들은 되었습니다 사탄의 노예들이

and they became the slaves of Satan.

그들은 시작했습니다 생각하기를 / 행동하기를 / 그리고 말하기를 / 사탄처럼

They started to think, / act, / and speak / like Satan.

그들은 가졌습니다 사탄의 마음을

They had the mind of Satan.

그것은 불립니다 "죄성"이라고

It is called "sinful nature."

Caption

Unit 13

Chunk by Chunk

Words Note

- [ ] **human** [hjú:mən] 인간, 사람

- [ ] **pollute** [pəlú:t] 더럽히다, 오염시키다

- [ ] **sin** [sin] 죄

- [ ] **live** [liv] 살다

- [ ] **the Holy God** 거룩하신 하나님

- [ ] **that is why** … 그것이 ~이유다

- [ ] **drive … out** ~를 몰아내다, 내쫓다

- [ ] **while** [hwail] ~하면서도, ~에 반하여

- [ ] **still** [stil] 여전히, 아직

- [ ] **love** [lʌv] 사랑하다

Trace and Write

인간은 죄에 의해 오염된 /

The human polluted by sin /

살 수 없었습니다 거룩하신 하나님과 함께

couldn't live with the Holy God.

그것이 이유였습니다 / 하나님께서 그들을 내쫓으신 /

That was why / God drove them out /

그분이 그들을 여전히 사랑하시면서도

while He still loved them.

Caption

Chapter 06

Are we also sinners? And what will happen to sinners?

Unit 14

Chunk by Chunk

Words Note

☐ **also** [ɔ́ːlsou] ~도 또한

☐ **sinner** [sínər] 죄인

☐ **happen to** ··· ~에게 일어나다

☐ **sinful** [sínfəl] 죄가 되는, 죄악의

☐ **nature** [néitʃər] 본성

☐ **descendant** [diséndənt] 후손

Trace and Write

우리도 또한 죄인들일까요

Are we also sinners?

그리고 무슨 일이 일어날까요 죄인들에게

And what will happen to sinners?

우리도 또한 죄인들일까요

Are we also sinners?

네 우리 모두 죄인들입니다

Yes. We are all sinners.

우리도 가지고 있습니다 죄성을 /

We also have sinful nature /

왜냐하면 우리는 후손들이기 때문입니다 / 아담과 이브의

because we are the descendants / of Adam and Eve.

Caption

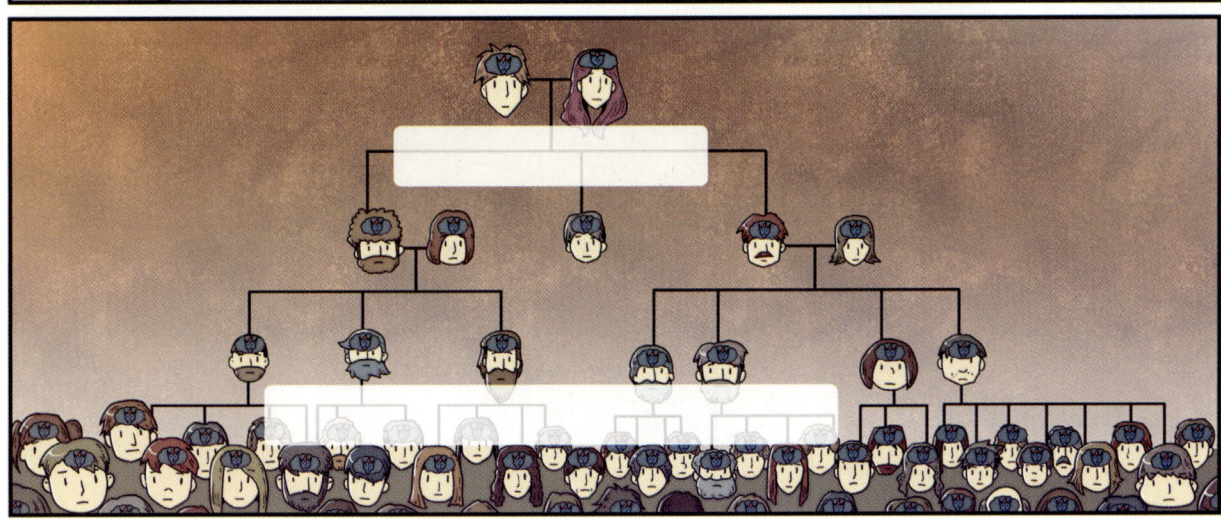

Unit 15

Chunk by Chunk

We have had sinful nature from birth,

and we sin against God every day.

If we go on living like this

and die with sin,

we will be judged

and thrown into Hell.

Words Note

- **sinful** [sínfəl] 죄가 되는, 죄악의

- **nature** [néitʃər] 본성

- **from birth** 태어날 때부터

- **sin against** … ~에게 죄를 짓다

- **go on** … ~ 하기를 계속하다

- **like** [laik] ~와 (똑)같이, ~처럼

- **die** [dai] 죽다

- **judge** [dʒʌdʒ] 심판하다

- **throw into** … ~에 던지다, 던져 넣다

Trace and Write

우리는 가지고 있어 왔습니다 죄성을 / 태어날 때부터 /

We have had sinful nature / from birth, /

그래서 우리는 하나님께 죄를 짓습니다 / 매일

and we sin against God / every day.

만일 우리가 계속 살아간다면 이와 같이 /

If we go on living like this /

그리고 죽는다면 죄와 함께 /

and die with sin, /

우리는 심판을 받게 될 것입니다 /

we will be judged /

그리고 던져질 것입니다 지옥 속으로

and thrown into Hell.

Caption

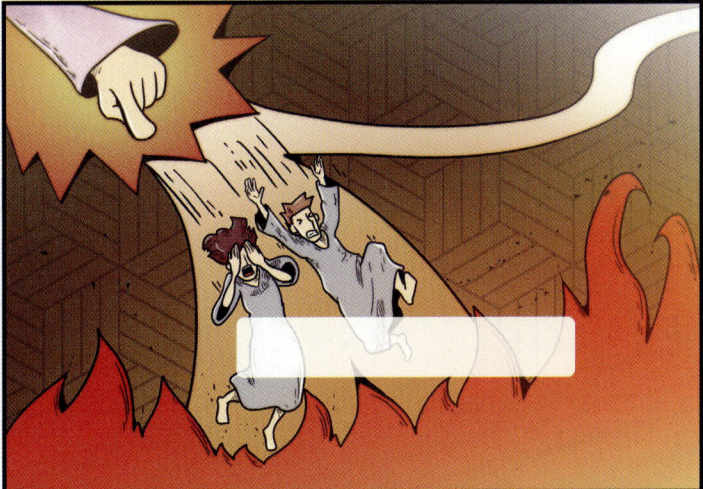

Chapter 07

What is Hell like?

Unit 16

Chunk by Chunk

Words Note

- [ ] **too … to …** ~하기에 너무 ~하다

- [ ] **horrible** [hɔ́:rəbl, hɔ́rəbl] 무서운, 끔찍한

- [ ] **describe** [diskráib] 묘사하다

- [ ] **place** [pleis] 장소, 곳

- [ ] **angel** [éindʒəl] 천사

- [ ] **betray** [bitréi] 배반하다, 배신하다

- [ ] **people** [pí:pl] 사람들

- [ ] **follow** [fálou] 따르다

- [ ] **throw into …** ~에 던지다, 던져 넣다

Trace and Write

지옥은 어떤 곳인가요

What is Hell like?

지옥은 너무나 무서운 곳입니다 / 묘사하기에

Hell is too horrible / to describe.

이곳은 그 장소였습니다 / 사탄과 그의 천사들을 위한 /

This was the place / for Satan and his angels /

하나님을 배신한

who betrayed God.

그러나 또한 / 사람들도 / 사탄을 따르는 /

But also / the people / who follow Satan /

던져집니다 지옥 속으로

are thrown into Hell.

Caption

Unit 17

Chunk by Chunk

Hell is a lake of fire.

In Hell, flesh-eating worms never die,

and the fire never goes out.

Everyone will be salted with fire.

You cannot take a sip of water

despite your burning thirst.

Words Note

- **lake** [leik] 호수; 연못

- **fire** [faiər] 불

- **flesh-eating worm** 살을 파먹는 벌레

- **never** [névər] 절대로 ~ 않다

- **die** [dai] 죽다

- **go out** (불꽃 등이) 꺼지다

- **everyone** [évriwʌn, -wən] 누구나, 모두

- **salt** [sɔːlt] ~에 절이다

- **take** [teik] (물, 음료 등을) 마시다

- **a sip of** … ~의 한 모금

- **despite** [dispáit] ~임에도 불구하고

- **burning** [bə́:rniŋ] 타오르는

- **thirst** [θə:rst] 갈증

Trace and Write

지옥은 불못입니다

Hell is a lake of fire.

지옥에서는 / 살을 파먹는 벌레들도 절대로 죽지 않습니다 /

In Hell, / flesh-eating worms never die, /

그리고 불은 절대로 꺼지지 않습니다

and the fire never goes out.

모든 사람들이 절여질 것입니다 불에

Everyone will be salted with fire.

당신은 마실 수 없습니다 한 모금의 물을 /
You cannot take a sip of water /

당신의 타오르는 갈증에도 불구하고
despite your burning thirst.

Caption

Unit 18

Chunk by Chunk

Words Note

- [ ] **once** [wʌns] 일단 ~하면

- [ ] **send** [send] ~에 보내다

- [ ] **late** [leit] 늦은

- [ ] **regret** [rigrét] 후회

- [ ] **scream** [skri:m] 소리치다

- [ ] **pain** [pein] 고통

- [ ] **want** [want, wɔ:nt] ~하기를 원하다, ~하고 싶다

- [ ] **die** [dai] 죽다

- [ ] **stay** [stei] 머무르다

- [ ] **forever** [fəreˈvər] 영원히

Trace and Write

일단 당신이 보내지면 지옥으로 /

Once you are sent to Hell, /

너무 늦습니다 후회하기에

it is too late for regrets.

당신은 소리칠 것입니다 큰 고통 속에서 /

You will scream in great pain /

그리고 당신은 죽기를 원합니다 /

and you want to die, /

그러나 당신은 그럴 수 없습니다

but you can't.

당신은 머물러야만 합니다 거기에서 영원히

You have to stay there forever.

Caption

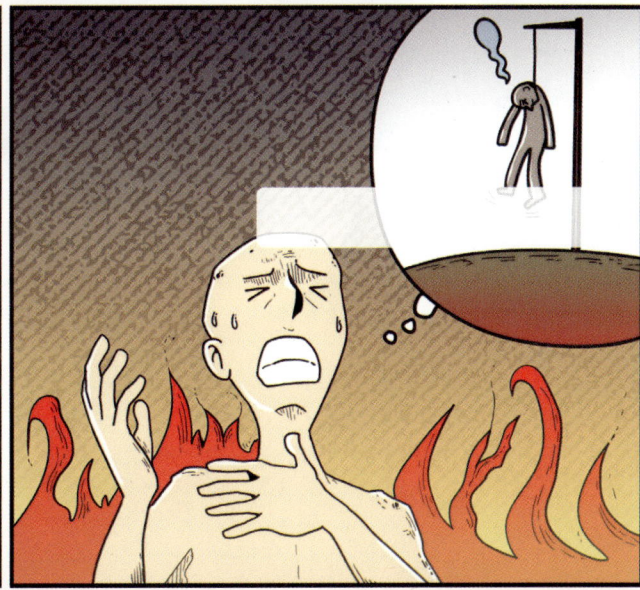

Chapter

08

Then, what is Heaven like?

Unit 19

Chunk by Chunk

Words Note

- **live** [liv] 살다

- **happily** [hǽpili] 행복하게

- **decorate ··· with ···** ~을 ~으로 장식하다

- **various** [vέəriəs] 온갖, 다양한

- **jewel** [dʒúːəl] 보석

- **flow** [flou] (물 등이) 흐르다

- **river** [rívər] 강

- **the water of life** 생명수

- **clear** [kliər] 맑은

- **crystal** [krístl] 수정

Trace and Write

그러면 / 천국은 어떤 곳일까요

Then, / what is Heaven like?

천국은 / 당신이 살 수 있는 곳입니다 /

Heaven is / where you can live /

하나님과 예수님과 함께 / 행복하게 영원히

with God and Jesus / happily forever.

그곳은 장식되어 있습니다 다양한 보석들로

It is decorated with various jewels.

그곳에는 강이 흐릅니다 / 생명수의 /

There flows the river / of the water of life /

수정같이 맑은

as clear as crystal.

Caption

Unit 20

Chunk by Chunk

The trees of life on the riversides bear fruit every month.

There is no curse

and no sadness.

Also, there is no darkness,

for God gives you light.

Words Note

- **the tree of life** 생명나무

- **riverside** [rívərsàid] 강가

- **bear** [bɛər] (열매 등을) 맺다

- **fruit** [fruːt] 열매

- **month** [mʌnθ] (달력의) 달

- **curse** [kəːrs] 저주

- **sadness** [sǽdnis] 슬픔

- **darkness** [dάːrknis] 어둠

- **give** [giv] 주다

- **light** [lait] 빛

Trace and Write

생명나무들은 / 강가에 있는 /

The trees of life / on the riversides /

열매를 맺습니다 / 매달

bear fruit / every month.

저주가 없습니다 / 그리고 슬픔이 없습니다

There is no curse / and no sadness.

또한 / 어둠이 없습니다 /

Also, / there is no darkness, /

왜냐하면 하나님이 당신에게 빛을 주시기 때문에

for God gives you light.

Caption

Unit 21

Chunk by Chunk

Words Note

☐ **see** [siː] 보다

☐ **worship** [wə́ːrʃip] ~에 대해 예배하다, 경배하다

☐ **everyone** [évriwʌn, -wən] 누구나, 모두

☐ **only** [óunli] 오직

☐ **one** [wʌn] (일반적인) 사람

☐ **name** [neim] 이름

☐ **the Book of Life** 생명책

☐ **enter** [éntər] 들어가다, 들어오다

Trace and Write

당신은 볼 수 있습니다 / 그리고 경배할 수 있습니다 / 하나님과 예수님을

You can see / and worship / God and Jesus.

그러나 / 모든 사람이 / 천국으로 갈 수 있는 것은 아닙니다

But, / not everyone / can go to Heaven.

오직 그 사람들만 /

Only the ones /

그들의 이름들이 / 생명책에 있는 /

whose names are / in the Book of Life /

천국에 들어갈 수 있습니다

can enter Heaven.

Caption

Chapter 09

What do people do to go to Heaven instead of Hell?

Unit 22

Chunk by Chunk

Words Note

- [ ] **instead of** ··· ~ 대신에

- [ ] **be afraid of** ··· ~을 두려워하다

- [ ] **avoid** [əvɔ́id] ~하기를 피하다

- [ ] **do** [du, də; (강) duː] (행위 등을) 하다, 행하다

- [ ] **thing** [θiŋ] (추상적으로 막연한) 것, 일

- [ ] **such as** ··· ~와 같은

- [ ] **donate** [dóuneit] ~에 기부하다

- [ ] **charity** [tʃǽrəti] 자선단체

- [ ] **help** [help] 돕다

- [ ] **the poor** 불쌍한 사람들, 가난한 사람들

Trace and Write

무엇을 사람들은 할까요 /

What do people do /

_____

천국으로 가려고 / 지옥 대신에

to go to Heaven / instead of Hell?

_____

사람들은 두려워합니다 지옥을

People are afraid of Hell.

_____

_____

_____

피하기 위해 지옥으로 가는 것을 /

To avoid going to Hell /

_____

_____

_____

그리고 천국으로 가기 위해 /

and to go to Heaven, /

_____

_____

_____

그들은 합니다 많은 일들을

they do many things.

그들은 합니다 좋은 일들을

They do good things /

돈을 기부하는 것과 같은 자선 단체에 /

such as donating money to charity /

그리고 불쌍한 사람들을 돕는

and helping the poor.

Caption

Gospel Questions

1. What is Heaven like?

2. What do people do to go to Heaven?

Unit 23

Chunk by Chunk

Words Note

- **do** [du, də; (강) du:] (행위 등을) 하다, 행하다

- **meditation** [mèdətéiʃən] 명상

- **suffering** [sʌfəriŋ] 고행

- **religious** [rilídʒəs] 종교의

- **thing** [θiŋ] (추상적으로 막연한) 것, 일

- **enough** [inʌf] 충분한, 족한

Trace and Write

또는 그들은 명상을 합니다 / 그리고 고행을

Or they do meditation / and suffering.

또는 그들은 합니다 종교적인 일들을

Or they do religious things.

하지만 / 이것들은 충분하지 않습니다 /

But / these are not enough /

그들이 / 천국으로 가기에는

for them / to go to Heaven.

Caption

Chapter 10

Then,
how could people
be forgiven?

Unit 24

Chunk by Chunk

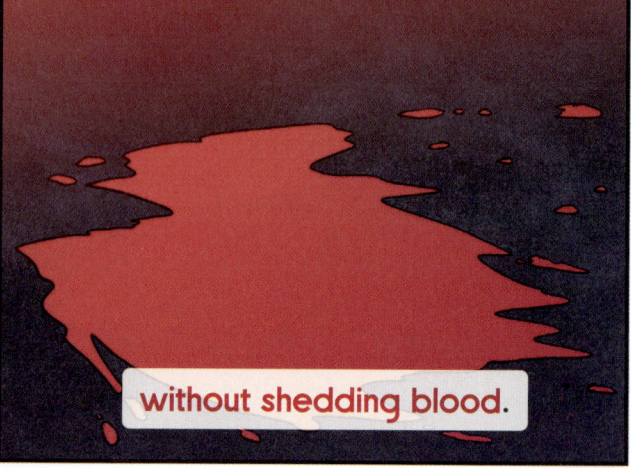

Words Note

☐ **forgive** [fərgív] 용서하다, 사하다 *forgiveness [fərgívnis] 용서, 죄를 사함

☐ **sin** [sin] 죄를 짓다; 죄

☐ **make** [meik] (행위 등을) 하다, 행하다

☐ **offering** [ɔ́:fəriŋ] (신에 대한) 공물, 제물 (sacrifice)

☐ **kill** [kil] 죽이다

☐ **animal** [ǽnəməl] 동물

☐ **sacrifice** [sǽkrəfàis] (산) 제물, 속죄제물

☐ **without** [wiðáut, wiθáut] (~함이) 없이

☐ **shed** [ʃed] (피 등을) 흘리다

☐ **blood** [blʌd] 피

Trace and Write

그러면 / 어떻게 사람들은 용서받을 수 있었나요

Then, / how could people be forgiven?

옛날에는 /

In the old days, /

하나님이 사람들에게 허락하셨습니다 / 죄를 지은 /

God let those / who sinned /

속죄제를 올리도록

make sin offerings.

사람들은 죽였습니다 동물을 /

People killed an animal /

속죄제물로서 / 그들의 죄들에 대한

as a sacrifice / for their sins.

왜냐하면 용서가 없기 때문입니다 /

For there is no forgiveness /

피 흘림 없이는

without shedding blood.

Caption

Gospel Questions

1. Who made sin offerings?

2. Why did they kill an animal as a sacrifice for their sins?

Unit 25

Chunk by Chunk

However, as time went by,

the offering became formal rituals

with no true repentance.

In the end, God hated this meaningless ritual.

This animal sin offering could not be an ultimate solution.

Words Note

☐ **however** [hauévər] 그러나, 그렇지만

☐ **go by** (시간이) 경과하다

☐ **offering** [ɔ́:fəriŋ] (신에 대한) 공물, 제물 (sacrifice)

☐ **become** [bikʌ́m] ~이 되다

☐ **formal** [fɔ́:rməl] 형식적인

☐ **ritual** [rítʃuəl] 의식, 의례

☐ **true** [tru:] 진정한, 참된

☐ **repentance** [ripéntəns] 회개, 참회

☐ **in the end** 결국, 마지막에는

☐ **hate** [heit] 싫어하다

☐ **meaningless** [míːniŋlis] 의미 없는

☐ **ultimate** [ʌ́ltəmət] 궁극적인

☐ **solution** [səlúːʃən] 해결책

Trace and Write

그러나 / 시간이 흐르면서 /

However, / as time went by, / _____

_____

_____

그 제사는 되었습니다 형식적인 의례가 /

the offering became formal rituals / _____

_____

_____

진정한 회개가 없는

with no true repentance. _____

_____

_____

결국 /

In the end, / _____

_____

_____

하나님은 싫어하셨습니다 / 이런 의미없는 의식을

God hated / this meaningless ritual. _____

_____

_____

이 동물 속죄제는 /

This animal sin offering /

될 수 없었습니다 궁극적인 해결책이

could not be an ultimate solution.

Caption

Chapter 11

What was God's plan?

Unit 26

Chunk by Chunk

Words Note

- **plan** [plæn] 계획

- **send** [send] ~을 보내다

- **one and only** 유일한

- **son** [sʌn] 아들

- **great** [greit] 큰, 위대한

- **sacrifice** [sǽkrəfàis] (산) 제물, 속죄제물

- **conceive** [kənsíːv] (아이를) 가지다, 임신하다

- **the Holy Spirit** 성령

- **be born of …** ~에서 태어나다

- **the Virgin Mary** 동정녀 마리아

Trace and Write

무엇이 하나님의 계획이었을까요
What was God's plan?

하나님은 보내셨습니다 / 그분의 외아들을 /
God sent / His one and only Son /

위대한 속죄제물로서
as a great sacrifice.

그분은 예수님이셨습니다
He was Jesus.

그분은 잉태되셨습니다 성령님에 의해 /
He was conceived by the Holy Spirit /

그리고 태어나셨습니다 동정녀 마리아에게서
and born of the Virgin Mary.

Caption

Unit 27

Chunk by Chunk

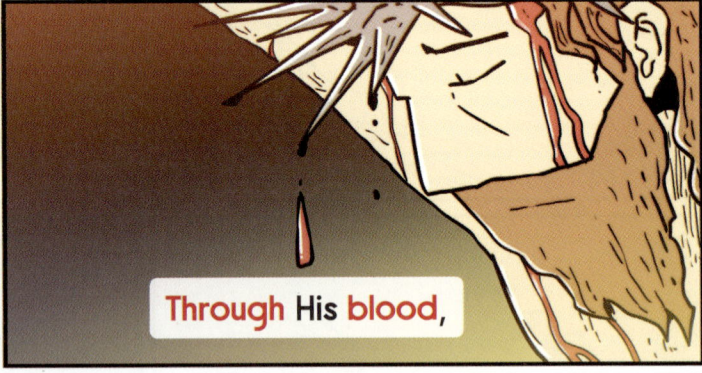

Words Note

☐ **teach** [tiːtʃ] 가르치다

☐ **gospel** [gɑ́spəl] (the gospel) 복음

☐ **perform** [pərfɔ́ːrm] (일 등을) 행하다

☐ **miracle** [mírəkl] 기적

☐ **although** [ɔːlðóu] 비록 ~이지만

☐ **sinless** [sínlis] 죄 없는

☐ **crucify** [krúːsəfài] 십자가에 못박다, 처형하다

☐ **shed** [ʃed] (피 등을) 흘리다

☐ **blood** [blʌd] 피

- [ ] **cross** [krɔːs] 십자가

- [ ] **people** [píːpl] 사람들

- [ ] **through** [θruː] ~을 통하여

- [ ] **forgive** [fərgív] 용서하다, 사하다

Trace and Write

그분은 가르치셨습니다 복음을 /

He taught the gospel /

그리고 행하셨습니다 많은 기적들을

and performed many miracles.

예수님은 죄가 없으셨음에도 불구하고 /

Although Jesus was sinless, /

그분은 처형당하셨습니다 / 피를 흘리면서 /

He was crucified / shedding blood /

십자가에서 / 그분의 사람들을 위해

on the cross / for His people.

그분의 피를 통하여 /

Through His blood, /

우리는 용서받을 수 있었습니다 /

we could be forgiven /

그래서 천국으로 갈 수 있었습니다

and could go to Heaven.

Caption

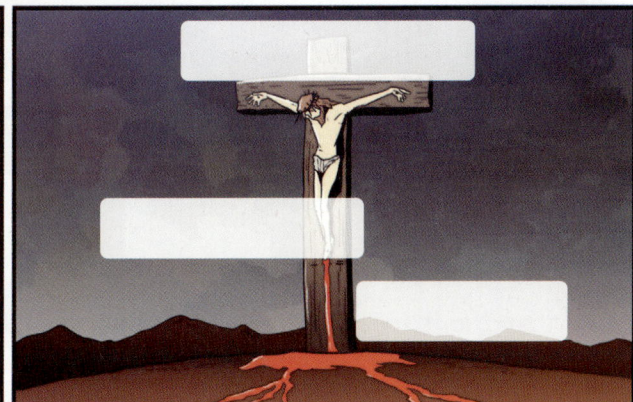

Chapter 12

What happened to Jesus after that?

Unit 28

Audio

Chunk by Chunk

On the third day,

He defeated death

and rose from the dead.

He showed Himself to the disciples.

And He told them about the kingdom of God.

After forty days,

He went up to Heaven.

Words Note

☐ **happen to** … ~에게 일어나다

☐ **after** [ǽftər] ~ 후에

☐ **third** [θəːrd] 셋째의, 세 번째, 사흘 째

☐ **defeat** [difíːt] 이기다, 패배시키다

☐ **death** [deθ] 죽음

☐ **rise** [raiz] (문어) [죽음에서] 다시 살아나다

☐ **the dead** 죽은 사람들

☐ **show** [ʃou] 보이다, 보여주다

☐ **himself** [imsélf; (강) him-] 그 자신, 그 스스로

☐ **disciple** [disáipl] (예수님의) 제자

☐ **tell** [tel] 말하다

☐ **the kingdom of God** 하나님의 나라

☐ **forty** [fɔ́ːrti] 40, 사십

☐ **go up** 올라가다

Trace and Write

무슨 일이 예수님께 일어났나요 / 그 후에

What happened to Jesus / after that?

사흘 째 되는 날에 /

On the third day, /

그분은 죽음을 이기셨습니다 /

He defeated death /

그리고 다시 살아나셨습니다 죽은 자들 가운데서

and rose from the dead.

그분은 자신을 나타내셨습니다 제자들에게

He showed Himself to the disciples.

그리고 그분은 그들에게 말씀하셨습니다 / 하나님의 나라에 대해

And he told them / about the kingdom of God.

사십일 후에 /

After forty days, /

그분은 올라가셨습니다 천국으로

He went up to Heaven.

Caption

Unit 29

Chunk by Chunk

Words Note

- [ ] **sit** [sit] 앉다

- [ ] **on the right hand of** ··· ~의 오른쪽 편에, 우편에

- [ ] **come** [kʌm] 오다

- [ ] **judge** [dʒʌdʒ] 심판하다

- [ ] **the living** 산 자들

- [ ] **the dead** 죽은 자들

- [ ] **know** [nou] 알다

- [ ] **exact** [igzækt] 정확한

- [ ] **time** [taim] 시간, 때

- [ ] **soon** [suːn] 곧

Trace and Write

그분은 앉아 계십니다 /

He is sitting /

하나님의 오른쪽 편에 지금

on the right hand of God now.

그분은 오실 것입니다 다시 /

He will come again /

심판하기 위해 산 자들과 죽은 자들을

to judge the living and the dead.

아무도 모릅니다 정확한 때를 /

Nobody knows the exact time. /

그러나 그분은 오실 것입니다 곧

but He will come soon.

Caption

Chapter 13

Then,
what should I do?

Unit 30

Chunk by Chunk

Words Note

- [ ] **say** [sei] 말하다

- [ ] **receive** [risíːv] 받아들이다, 영접하다

- [ ] **believe in** … ~를 믿다

- [ ] **name** [neim] 이름

- [ ] **give** [giv] 주다

- [ ] **right** [rait] 권리

- [ ] **become** [bikʌm] ~이 되다

- [ ] **children** [tʃíldrən] 아이들, 자녀들 (child의 복수형)

- [ ] **whoever** [huːévər] 누구든지

- [ ] **accept** [æksépt] 받아들이다, 맞아들이다

Trace and Write

그러면 / 무엇을 나는 해야 하나요

Then, / what should I do?

성경은 말합니다 / 요한복음 1장 12절에서 /

The Bible says / in John 1:12, /

모두에게 / 그분을 영접한 /

"To all / who did receive Him, /

사람들에게 / 그분의 이름을 믿는 /

to those / who believed in His name, /

그분은 권리를 주셨다 /

He gave the right /

하나님의 자녀들이 되는
to become children of God."

그래서 / 누구든지 예수님을 믿고 /
So, / whoever believes in Jesus /

그분을 받아들이는 자는 /
and accepts Him /

될 수 있습니다 하나님의 자녀가
can be a child of God.

Caption

Gospel Questions

1. Is everyone a child of God?

2. What should I do to become a child of God?

Unit **31**

Chunk by Chunk

 Audio

Words Note

- [ ] **call** [kɔːl] 부르다

- [ ] **father** [fάːðər] 아버지

- [ ] **take care of** … ~을 돌보다

- [ ] **receive** [risíːv] 받아들이다, 영접하다

- [ ] **do** [du, də; (강) duː] (행위 등을) 하다, 행하다

- [ ] **truly** [trúːli] 진심으로, 진실되게

- [ ] **believe in** … ~를 믿다

- [ ] **confess** [kənfés] 고백하다

- [ ] **lord** [lɔːrd] (보통 … Lord) 주(님)

- [ ] **mouth** [mauθ] 입

Trace and Write

그들은 하나님을 부를 수 있습니다 "아버지"라고

They can call God "Father."

그리고 그분은 돌보십니다 그들을

And He takes care of them.

그러면 / 예수님을 영접하기 위해서 /

Then, / to receive Jesus, /

무엇을 당신은 해야만 하나요

what must you do?

당신은 진심으로 믿어야 합니다 그분을

You must truly believe in Him.

당신은 고백해야 합니다 / "예수님은 나의 주님이시다"라고 /

You must confess / "Jesus is my Lord" /

당신의 입으로

with your mouth.

Caption

Gospel Questions

1. Who is God, and what is He like?

2. What must you do to receive Jesus?

Unit 32

Chunk by Chunk

And, Jesus will come into you

and become your Lord.

You will become a child of God

and live in Heaven forever.

Now, Jesus is standing at your door

and knocking.

He is waiting

for you to open the door of your heart.

Words Note

- **come into** … ~에 들어오다

- **become** [bikʌm] ~이 되다

- **lord** [lɔːrd] (보통 … Lord) 주(님)

- **child** [tʃaild] 아이, 자녀

- **live** [liv] 살다

- **forever** [fəreˈvər] 영원히

- **stand** [stænd] 서 있다

- **door** [dɔːr] 문

- **knock** [nak] (문 등을) 똑똑 두드리다

☐ **wait** [weit] 기다리다

☐ **open** [óupən] (문 등을) 열다

☐ **heart** [hɑːrt] 마음

Trace and Write

그러면 / 예수님은 오십니다 당신 안으로 /

And, / Jesus will come into you /

_____

_____

그리고 되십니다 당신의 주님이

and become your Lord.

_____

_____

당신은 될 것입니다 하나님의 자녀가 /

You will become a child of God /

_____

_____

그리고 살 것입니다 천국에서 영원히

and live in Heaven forever.

_____

_____

지금 / 예수님은 서 계십니다 / 당신의 문에서 /

Now, / Jesus is standing / at your door /

_____

_____

그리고 두드리고 계십니다
and knocking.

그분은 기다리고 계십니다 /
He is waiting /

당신이 / 당신의 마음의 문을 열기를
for you / to open the door of your heart.

Caption

Chapter

14

The Salvation Prayer

Unit 33

Chunk by Chunk

Words Note

- [ ] **salvation** [sælvéiʃən] 구원

- [ ] **prayer** [prɛər] 기도; 기도 문구, 기도문 *pray [prei] 기도하다

- [ ] **important** [impɔ́:rtənt] 중요한

- [ ] **receive** [risíːv] 받아들이다, 영접하다

- [ ] **lord** [lɔːrd] (보통 … Lord) 주(님)

- [ ] **out loud** 큰 소리로, 소리 내어

- [ ] **true** [truː] 진실한

- [ ] **heart** [hɑːrt] 마음

- [ ] **father** [fɑ́ːðər] 아버지

☐ **sinner** [sínər] 죄인 *sin [sin] 죄

☐ **know** [nou] 알다

☐ **live** [liv] 살다

☐ **commit** [kəmít] (죄 등을) 저지르다, 범하다

☐ **realize** [ríːəlàiz] 깨닫다

☐ **die** [dai] 죽다

☐ **cross** [krɔːs] 십자가

Trace and Write

영접 기도문
The Salvation Prayer

이것은 / 매우 중요한 기도입니다 /
This is / the very important prayer /

예수님을 영접하는 / 당신의 주님으로
to receive Jesus / as your Lord.

기도하십시오 큰 소리로 / 당신의 진실한 마음을 다해서
Pray out loud / with all your true heart.

아버지 / 저는 죄인입니다
Father, / I am a sinner.

알지 못한 채 / 무엇을 위해 제가 살아가고 있는지 /
Not knowing / what I am living for. /

저는 저질러 왔습니다 많은 죄들을
I have committed many sins.

이제 / 저는 깨달았습니다 /
Now, / I realized /

예수님이 돌아가셨다는 것을 / 십자가에서 / 저의 죄들을 대신하여
that Jesus died / on the cross / for my sins.

Caption

Unit 34

Audio

Chunk by Chunk

Words Note

☐ **repent** [ripént] 회개하다

☐ **sin** [sin] 죄

☐ **wash … away** (죄 등을) 씻어 깨끗이 하다

☐ **blood** [blʌd] 피

☐ **thank you for …** ~해 줘서 감사하다

☐ **save** [seiv] 구하다, 구원하다

☐ **open** [óupən] 열다

☐ **heart** [ha:rt] 마음

☐ **receive** [risí:v] 받아들이다, 영접하다

☐ **lord** [lɔ:rd] (보통 … Lord) 주(님)

Trace and Write

저는 회개합니다 저의 모든 죄들을

I repent all my sins.

그것들을 깨끗이 씻어내 주시옵소서 / 그분의 피로

Please wash them away / with His blood.

예수님 / 감사합니다 저를 구원해 주셔서

Jesus, / thank You for saving me.

지금 / 저는 엽니다 저의 마음을

Now / I open my heart.

그리고 저는 당신을 영접합니다 / 저의 주님으로

And I receive You / as my Lord.

Caption

Unit 35

  Audio

Chunk by Chunk

Words Note

- **from now on** 지금부터, 이제부터

- **follow** [fálou] 따르다

- **serve** [sə:rv] 섬기다, 봉사하다

- **forever** [fəreˈvər] 영원히

- **guide** [gaid] 인도하다

- **make** [meik] (사람, 사물을) ~로 만들다

- **faithful** [féiθfəl] 충직한, 충실한

- **servant** [sə́:rvənt] 종, 하인

- **name** [neim] 이름

- **pray** [prei] 기도하다

Trace and Write

지금부터 /

From now on, /

저는 따르겠습니다 / 그리고 섬기겠습니다 당신을 영원히

I will follow / and serve You forever.

저를 인도해 주세요 /

Please guide me /

그리고 저를 만들어 주세요 당신의 충직한 종으로

and make me Your faithful servant.

예수님의 이름으로 / 기도합니다

In the name of Jesus, / I pray.

아멘

Amen.

Caption

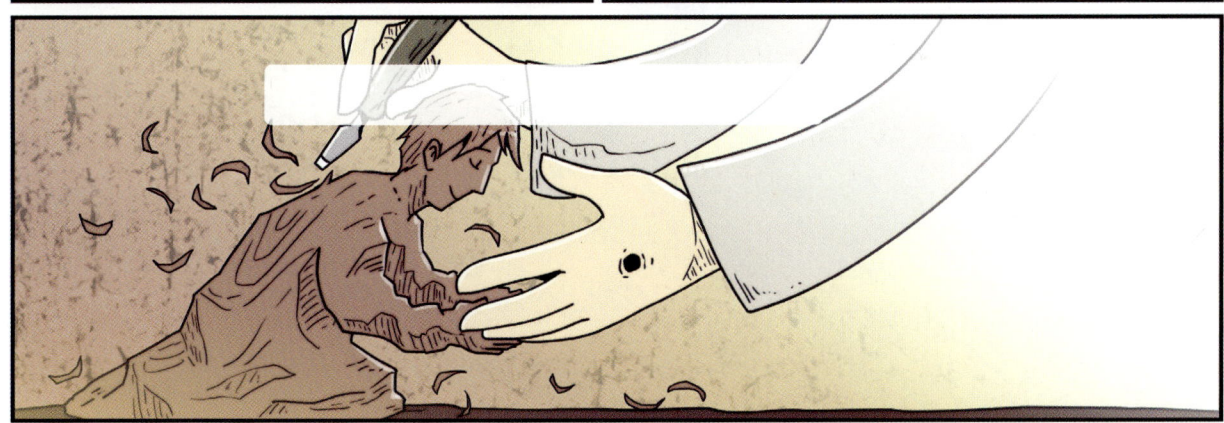

Chapter 15

Then, what should I do from now on?

Unit 36

Chunk by Chunk

Words Note

- **congratulations** 축하합니다

- **sin** [sin] 죄

- **forgive** [fərgív] 용서하다, 사하다

- **become** [bikʌm] ~이 되다

- **child** [tʃaild] 아이, 자녀

- **name** [neim] 이름

- **write** [rait] 쓰다, 기록하다

- **the Book of Life** 생명책

- **live** [liv] 살다

- **forever** [fərevər] 영원히

Trace and Write

그러면 / 무엇을 저는 해야 하나요 / 이제부터

Then, / what should I do / from now on?

축하합니다

Congratulations!

이제 / 당신의 모든 죄들은 용서받았습니다

Now, / all your sins have been forgiven.

당신은 되었습니다 하나님의 자녀가

You have become a child of God.

또한 / 당신의 이름은 기록되었습니다 /
Also, / your name has been written /

생명책에
in the Book of Life.

당신은 살 것입니다 천국에서 영원히
You will live in Heaven forever.

Caption

Gospel Questions

1. What must I do to receive forgiveness from God?

2. What does it mean to become a child of God?

Unit 37

Chunk by Chunk

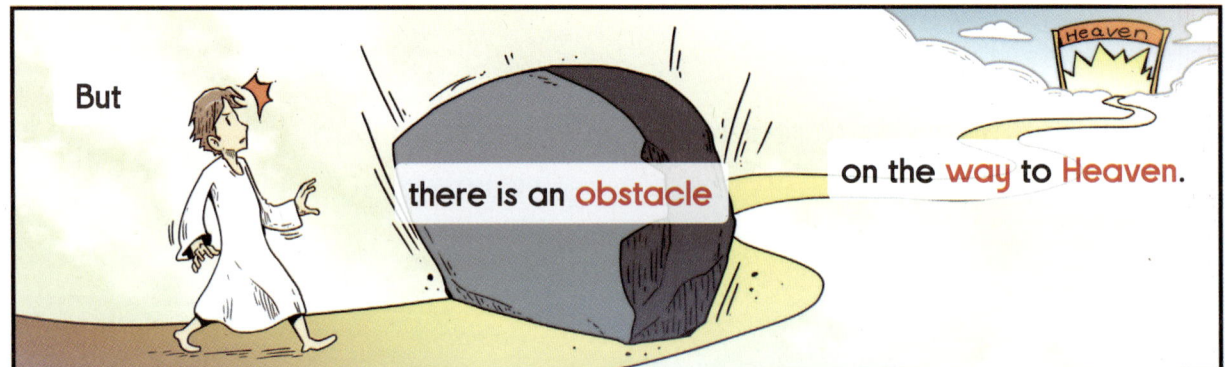

Words Note

- **obstacle** [άbstəkl] 장애물, 방해물

- **on the way to …** ~로 가는 길에, 도중에

- **trick** [trik] 속이다

- **constantly** [kάnstəntli] 끊임없이, 계속

- **tempt** [tempt] 유혹하다

- **mean** [mi:n] (보통 means) 수단, 방법, 방도

- **alone** [əlóun] 혼자, 홀로

- **easy** [í:zi] 쉬운

- **target** [tá:rgit] (공격의) 표적

Trace and Write

그러나 / 방해물이 있습니다 /

But / there is an obstacle /

___

___

___

가는 길에 천국으로

on the way to Heaven.

___

___

___

그것은 사탄입니다 /

That is "Satan /

___

___

___

속였던 아담과 이브를

who tricked Adam and Eve."

___

___

___

사탄은 끊임없이 우리를 유혹합니다 /

Satan constantly tempts us /

모든 수단을 다해서

by all means.

그리고 / 혼자서는 /

And, / alone, /

당신은 될 수 있습니다 쉬운 표적이 / 사탄에게

you can be an easy target / for Satan.

Caption

Gospel Questions

1. Who is Satan, and what is he like?

2. Why does Satan constantly tempt us?

Unit 38

Chunk by Chunk

Words Note

☐ **therefore** [ðέərfɔ̀ːr] 그러므로

☐ **believer** [bilíːvər] (종교를) 믿는 사람, 신자

☐ **get together** 모이다

☐ **read** [riːd] 읽다

☐ **the Bible** 성경

☐ **obey** [oubéi] 따르다, 순종하다

☐ **God's words** 하나님의 말씀

☐ **pray** [prei] 기도하다

☐ **love** [lʌv] 사랑하다

- [ ] **one another** 서로

- [ ] **live** [liv] 살다

- [ ] **different** [difərənt] 다른, 구별된

- [ ] **life** [laif] 삶

Trace and Write

그러므로 /

Therefore, /

모든 믿는 사람들은 모여야 합니다

all believers should get together.

우리는 읽어야 합니다 성경을 /

We must read the Bible /

그리고 따라야 합니다 하나님의 말씀을

and obey God's words.

우리는 기도해야 합니다 /

We must pray /

그리고 사랑해야 합니다 서로

and love one another.

우리는 살아야 합니다 다른 삶을 / 사탄의 것과

We must live different lives / from Satan's.

Caption

Chapter 16

Where should we go?

Unit 39

Chunk by Chunk

You must go to church right away.

Church is the "Community of Faith"

where God's people gather.

In the community,

Jesus becomes the head

and all church members become His body.

Words Note

- **church** [tʃəːrtʃ] 교회

- **right away** 즉시, 바로

- **community** [kəmjúːnəti] 공동체

- **faith** [feiθ] 믿음

- **gather** [gǽðər] (사람들이) 모이다

- **become** [bikʌ́m] ~이 되다

- **head** [hed] 머리

- **member** [mémbər] 구성원

- **body** [bɑ́di] 몸

Trace and Write

어디로 우리는 가야 하나요

Where should we go?

당신은 가야 합니다 교회로 / 즉시

You must go to church / right away.

교회는 / 믿음의 공동체입니다 /

Church is / the "Community of Faith" /

하나님의 사람들이 모이는

where God's people gather.

그 공동체에서 /

In the community, /

예수님은 되십니다 머리가 /

Jesus becomes the head /

그리고 모든 교회 구성원들은 / 됩니다 그분의 몸이

and all church members / become His body.

Caption

Gospel Questions

1. What is the church?

2. Why is it important to go to church?

Unit 40

Chunk by Chunk

In the church,

there are words of God

and fellowship with believers.

There are works of the Holy Spirit

and forgiveness of sins.

There are answers to the prayers

and praises of joy.

When we march to Heaven together as one body in Christ,

God will bless us.

Words Note

- **church** [tʃəːrtʃ] 교회

- **words of God** 하나님의 말씀

- **fellowship** [feˈlouʃiˌp] 교제, 유대감

- **believer** [bilíːvər] (종교를) 믿는 사람, 신자

- **work** [wəːrk] 일, 역사

- **the Holy Spirit** 성령

- **forgiveness** [fərgívnis] 용서, 죄를 사함

- **sin** [sin] 죄

- **answer** [ǽnsər] 응답, 대답

- [ ] **prayer** [prɛər] 기도

- [ ] **praise** [preiz] 찬양

- [ ] **joy** [dʒɔi] 기쁨

- [ ] **march** [mɑːrtʃ] 행진하다

- [ ] **together** [təgéðər] 함께, 같이

- [ ] **body** [bádi] 몸

- [ ] **bless** [bles] 축복하다

Trace and Write

교회에는 /

In the church, /

있습니다 하나님의 말씀이 /

there are words of God /

그리고 성도들의 교제가

and fellowship with believers.

있습니다 성령님의 역사가 /

There are works of the Holy Spirit /

그리고 죄의 용서가

and forgiveness of sins.

있습니다 기도들에 대한 응답들이 /
There are answers to the prayers /

그리고 기쁨의 찬양들이
and praises of joy.

우리가 천국으로 행진할 때 함께 /
When we march to Heaven together /

한 몸으로 그리스도 안에서 /
as one body in Christ. /

하나님은 축복하실 것입니다 우리를
God will bless us.

Caption

Appendix A

The Lord's Prayer

The Apostles' Creed

The Lord's Prayer

Audio

The Apostles' Creed

Audio

BIBLE
NOTE

Who made the world?

* **Genesis 1:1** In the beginning God created the heavens and the earth.

* **Genesis 1:4-5** ⁴God saw that the light was good, and he separated the light from the darkness. ⁵God called the light "day", and the darkness he called "night". And there was evening, and there was morning — the first day.

* **Genesis 1:6-10** ⁶And God said, "Let there be a vault between the waters to separate water from water." ⁷So God made the vault and separated the water under the vault from the water above it. And it was so. ⁸God called the vault "sky". And there was evening, and there was morning — the second day. ⁹And God said, "Let the water under the sky be gathered to one place, and let dry ground appear." And it was so. ¹⁰God called the dry ground "land", and the gathered waters he called "seas." And God saw that it was good.

* **Genesis 1:11-12** ¹¹Then God said, "Let the land produce vegetation: seed-bearing plants and trees on the land that bear fruit with seed in it, according to their various kinds." And it was so. ¹²The land produced vegetation: plants bearing seed according to their kinds and trees bearing fruit with seed in it according to their kinds. And God saw that it was good.

* **Genesis 1:14-18** ¹⁴And God said, "Let there be lights in the vault of the sky to separate the day from the night, and let them serve as signs to mark sacred times, and days and years, ¹⁵and let them be lights in the vault of the sky to give light on the earth." And it was so. ¹⁶God made two great lights — the greater light to govern the day and the lesser light to govern the night. He also made the stars. ¹⁷God set them in the vault of the sky to give light on the earth, ¹⁸to govern the day and the night, and to separate light from darkness. And God saw that it was good.

* **Genesis 1:20-21** [20]And God said, "Let the water teem with living creatures, and let birds fly above the earth across the vault of the sky." [21]So God created the great creatures of the sea and every living thing with which the water teems and that moves about in it, according to their kinds, and every winged bird according to its kind. And God saw that it was good.

Why did God make mankind?

* **Genesis 1:27** So God created mankind in his own image, in the image of God he created them; male and female he created them.

* **Genesis 2:7** Then the LORD God formed a man from the dust of the ground and breathed into his nostrils the breath of life, and the man became a living being.

* **John 3:16** For God so loved the world that he gave his one and only Son, that whoever believes in him shall not perish but have eternal life.

* **Isaiah 43:1** But now, this is what the LORD says — he who created you, Jacob, he who formed you, Israel: "Do not fear, for I have redeemed you; I have summoned you by name; you are mine.

* **Isaiah 43:21** the people I formed for myself that they may proclaim my praise.

* **Genesis 1:28** God blessed them and said to them, "Be fruitful and increase in number; fill the earth and subdue it. Rule over the fish in the sea and the birds in the sky and over every living creature that moves on the ground."

What did they do wrong?

* **Genesis 2:16** And the LORD God commanded the man, "You are free to eat from any tree in the garden;

* **Genesis 2:17** but you must not eat from the tree of the knowledge of good and evil, for when you eat from it you will certainly die."

* **Genesis 3:4-5** ⁴"You will not certainly die," the serpent said to the woman. ⁵"For God knows that when you eat from it your eyes will be opened, and you will be like God, knowing good and evil."

* **Genesis 3:6** When the woman saw that the fruit of the tree was good for food and pleasing to the eye, and also desirable for gaining wisdom, she took some and ate it. She also gave some to her husband, who was with her, and he ate it.

What happened to Adam and Eve?

* **Genesis 3:16** To the woman he said, "I will make your pains in childbearing very severe; with painful labor you will give birth to children. Your desire will be for your husband, and he will rule over you."

* **Genesis 3:17, 19** ¹⁷To Adam he said, "Because you listened to your wife and ate fruit from the tree about which I commanded you, 'You must not eat from it,' "Cursed is the ground because of you; through painful toil you will eat food from it all the days of your life. ¹⁹By the sweat of your brow you will eat your food until you return to the ground, since from it you were taken;

* **Genesis 3:21** The LORD God made garments of skin for Adam and his wife and clothed them.

* **Genesis 3:23** So the LORD God banished him from the Garden of Eden to work the ground from which he had been taken.

 # Why did God punish them?

* **2 Corinthians 11:14** And no wonder, for Satan himself masquerades as an angel of light.

* **1 Timothy 5:15** Some have in fact already turned away to follow Satan.

* **Luke 22:3** Then Satan entered Judas, called Iscariot, one of the Twelve. (Similar verse: **John 13:27**)

* **John 8:34** Jesus replied, "Very truly I tell you, everyone who sins is a slave to sin.

* **2 Thessalonians 2:9** The coming of the lawless one will be in accordance with how Satan works. He will use all sorts of displays of power through signs and wonders that serve the lie,

* **Romans 7:17-19, 25** ^{17}As it is, it is no longer I myself who do it, but it is sin living in me. ^{18}For I know that good itself does not dwell in me, that is, in my sinful nature. For I have the desire to do what is good, but I cannot carry it out. ^{19}For I do not do the good I want to do but the evil I do not want to do — this I keep on doing. ^{25}... So then, I myself in my mind am a slave to God's law, but in my sinful nature a slave to the law of sin.

* **Isaiah 6:5** "Woe to me!" I cried, "I am ruined! For I am a man of unclean lips, and I live among a people of unclean lips, and my eyes have seen the King, the LORD Almighty."

 Are we also sinners? And what will happen to sinners?

* **Romans 3:10** As it is written: "There is no one righteous, not even one;

* **Romans 5:12** Therefore, just as sin entered the world through one man, and death through sin, and in this way death came to all people, because all sinned —

* **Romans 6:23** For the wages of sin is death ...

* **Revelation 20:12, 15** [12]And I saw the dead, great and small, standing before the throne, and books were opened. Another book was opened, which is the book of life. The dead were judged according to what they had done as recorded in the books. [15]Anyone whose name was not found written in the book of life was thrown into the lake of fire.

* **Hebrews 9:27** Just as people are destined to die once, and after that to face judgment,

* **James 1:15** Then, after desire has conceived, it gives birth to sin; and sin, when it is full-grown, gives birth to death.

What is Hell like?

* **Matthew 5:29-30** ^{29}If your right eye causes you to stumble, gouge it out and throw it away. It is better for you to lose one part of your body than for your whole body to be thrown into hell. ^{30}And if your right hand causes you to stumble, cut it off and throw it away. It is better for you to lose one part of your body than for your whole body to go into hell.

* **Matthew 10:28** Do not be afraid of those who kill the body but cannot kill the soul. Rather, be afraid of the One who can destroy both soul and body in hell. (Similar verse: **Luke 12:5**)

* **Matthew 25:41** "Then he will say to those on his left, 'Depart from me, you who are cursed, into the eternal fire prepared for the devil and his angels.

* **Matthew 13:50** and throw them into the blazing furnace, where there will be weeping and gnashing of teeth.

* **Revelation 19:20** But the beast was captured, and with it the false prophet who had performed the signs on its behalf. With these signs he had deluded those who had received the mark of the beast and worshiped its image. The two of them were thrown alive into the fiery lake of burning sulfur.

* **Revelation 20:14-15** ^{14}Then death and Hades were thrown into the lake of fire. The lake of fire is the second death. ^{15}Anyone whose name was not found written in the book of life was thrown into the lake of fire.

* **Revelation 21:8** But the cowardly, the unbelieving, the vile, the murderers, the sexually immoral, those who practice magic arts, the idolaters and all liars — they will be consigned to the fiery lake of burning sulfur. This is the second death."

* **Mark 9:48-49** ⁴⁸where "the worms that eat them do not die, and the fire is not quenched.' ⁴⁹Everyone will be salted with fire.

* **Luke 16:24** So he called to him, 'Father Abraham, have pity on me and send Lazarus to dip the tip of his finger in water and cool my tongue, because I am in agony in this fire.'

* **Luke 13:28** "There will be weeping there, and gnashing of teeth, when you see Abraham, Isaac and Jacob and all the prophets in the kingdom of God, but you yourselves thrown out.

* **Luke 16:28-31** ²⁸for I have five brothers. Let him warn them, so that they will not also come to this place of torment.' ²⁹"Abraham replied, 'They have Moses and the Prophets; let them listen to them.' ³⁰"'No, father Abraham,' he said, 'but if someone from the dead goes to them, they will repent.'" ³¹"He said to him, 'If they do not listen to Moses and the Prophets, they will not be convinced even if someone rises from the dead.'"

* **Revelation 14:11** And the smoke of their torment will rise for ever and ever. There will be no rest day or night for those who worship the beast and its image, or for anyone who receives the mark of its name."

* **2 Thessalonians 1:8-9** ⁸He will punish those who do not know God and do not obey the gospel of our Lord Jesus. ⁹They will be punished with everlasting destruction and shut out from the presence of the Lord and from the glory of his might

08 Then, what is Heaven like?

* **Revelation 4:2-3** ²At once I was in the Spirit, and there before me was a throne in heaven with someone sitting on it. ³And the one who sat there had the appearance of jasper and ruby. A rainbow that shone like an emerald encircled the throne.

* **John 14:2-3, 23** ²My Father's house has many rooms; if that were not so, would I have told you that I am going there to prepare a place for you? ³And if I go and prepare a place for you, I will come back and take you to be with me that you also may be where I am. ²³Jesus replied, "Anyone who loves me will obey my teaching. My Father will love them, and we will come to them and make our home with them.

* **Revelation 4:8-11** ⁸... "Holy, holy, holy is the Lord God Almighty,' who was, and is, and is to come." ⁹Whenever the living creatures give glory, honor and thanks to him who sits on the throne and who lives for ever and ever, ¹⁰the twenty-four elders fall down before him who sits on the throne and worship him who lives for ever and ever. They lay their crowns before the throne and say: ¹¹"You are worthy, our Lord and God, to receive glory and honor and power, for you created all things, and by your will they were created and have their being."

* **Revelation 21:11-27** ¹¹It shone with the glory of God, and its brilliance was like that of a very precious jewel, like a jasper, clear as crystal. ... ¹⁹The foundations of the city walls were decorated with every kind of precious stone. ... ²¹The twelve gates were twelve pearls, each gate made of a single pearl. The great street of the city was of gold, as pure as transparent glass. ... ²⁷Nothing impure will ever enter it, nor will anyone who does what is shameful or deceitful, but only those whose names are written in the Lamb's book of life.

* **Revelation 22:1** Then the angel showed me the river of the water of life, as clear as crystal, flowing from the throne of God and of the Lamb

* **Revelation 2:7** Whoever has ears, let them hear what the Spirit says to the churches. To the one who is victorious, I will give the right to eat from the tree of life, which is in the paradise of God.

* **Revelation 22:2** down the middle of the great street of the city. On each side of the river stood the tree of life, bearing twelve crops of fruit, yielding its fruit every month. And the leaves of the tree are for the healing of the nations.

* **Revelation 22:3** No longer will there be any curse. The throne of God and of the Lamb will be in the city, and his servants will serve him.

* **Revelation 21:25** On no day will its gates ever be shut, for there will be no night there.

* **Revelation 22:5** There will be no more night. They will not need the light of a lamp or the light of the sun, for the Lord God will give them light. And they will reign for ever and ever.

* **Matthew 5:20** For I tell you that unless your righteousness surpasses that of the Pharisees and the teachers of the law, you will certainly not enter the kingdom of heaven.

* **Matthew 7:21** "Not everyone who says to me, 'Lord, Lord,' will enter the kingdom of heaven, but only the one who does the will of my Father who is in heaven.

* **Matthew 19:24** Again I tell you, it is easier for a camel to go through the eye of a needle than for someone who is rich to enter the kingdom of God."
(Similar verses: **Mark 10:25**, **Luke 18:25**)

* **Matthew 24:39-42** ³⁹and they knew nothing about what would happen until the flood came and took them all away. That is how it will be at the coming of the Son of Man. ⁴⁰Two men will be in the field; one will be taken and the other left. ⁴¹Two women will be grinding with a hand mill; one will be taken and the other left. ⁴²"Therefore keep watch, because you do not know on what day your Lord will come.

* **Revelation 20:12, 15** ¹²And I saw the dead, great and small, standing before the throne, and books were opened. Another book was opened, which is the book of life. The dead were judged according to what they had done as recorded in the books. ¹⁵Anyone whose name was not found written in the book of life was thrown into the lake of fire.

What do people do to go to Heaven instead of Hell?

* **Matthew 10:28** Do not be afraid of those who kill the body but cannot kill the soul. Rather, be afraid of the One who can destroy both soul and body in hell. (Similar verse: **Luke 12:5**)

* **Romans 3:10-12** ¹⁰As it is written: "There is no one righteous, not even one; ¹¹there is no one who understands; there is no one who seeks God. ¹²All have turned away, they have together become worthless; there is no one who does good, not even one."

* **Romans 3:23** for all have sinned and fall short of the glory of God,

* **Ecclesiastes 7:20** Indeed, there is no one on earth who is righteous, no one who does what is right and never sins.

* **John 14:6** Jesus answered, "I am the way and the truth and the life. No one comes to the Father except through me.

Then, how could people be forgiven?

* **Leviticus 4:2-4** ²"Say to the Israelites: 'When anyone sins unintentionally and does what is forbidden in any of the LORD's commands — ³"'If the anointed priest sins, bringing guilt on the people, he must bring to the LORD a young bull without defect as a sin offering for the sin he has committed. ⁴He is to present the bull at the entrance to the tent of meeting before the LORD. He is to lay his hand on its head and slaughter it there before the LORD.

* **Hebrews 9:22** In fact, the law requires that nearly everything be cleansed with blood, and without the shedding of blood there is no forgiveness.

* **Isaiah 1:11-12** ¹¹"The multitude of your sacrifices — what are they to me?" says the LORD. "I have more than enough of burnt offerings, of rams and the fat of fattened animals; I have no pleasure in the blood of bulls and lambs and goats. ¹²When you come to appear before me, who has asked this of you, this trampling of my courts?

* **Hebrews 10:1-4, 8, 11** ¹The law is only a shadow of the good things that are coming — not the realities themselves. For this reason it can never, by the same sacrifices repeated endlessly year after year, make perfect those who draw near to worship. ²Otherwise, would they not have stopped being offered? For the worshipers would have been cleansed once for all, and would no longer have felt guilty for their sins. ³But those sacrifices are an annual reminder of sins. ⁴It is impossible for the blood of bulls and goats to take away sins. ⁸First he said,

"Sacrifices and offerings, burnt offerings and sin offerings you did not desire, nor were you pleased with them" — though they were offered in accordance with the law. ¹¹Day after day every priest stands and performs his religious duties; again and again he offers the same sacrifices, which can never take away sins.

* **Hebrews 10:6** with burnt offerings and sin offerings you were not pleased.

* **Hosea 6:6** For I desire mercy, not sacrifice, and acknowledgment of God rather than burnt offerings.

* **Isaiah 1:13** Stop bringing meaningless offerings! Your incense is detestable to me. New Moons, Sabbaths and convocations — I cannot bear your worthless assemblies.

* **1 Samuel 15:22** But Samuel replied: "Does the LORD delight in burnt offerings and sacrifices as much as in obeying the LORD? To obey is better than sacrifice, and to heed is better than the fat of rams.

* **Proverbs 21:3** To do what is right and just is more acceptable to the LORD than sacrifice.

11 What was God's plan?

* **Hebrews 9:11-12** ¹¹But when Christ came as high priest of the good things that are now already here, he went through the greater and more perfect tabernacle that is not made with human hands, that is to say, is not a part of this creation. ¹²He did not enter by means of the blood of goats and calves; but he entered the Most Holy Place once for all by his own blood, thus obtaining eternal redemption.

* **Hebrews 10:10** And by that will, we have been made holy through the sacrifice of the body of Jesus Christ once for all.

* **John 3:16** For God so loved the world that he gave his one and only Son, that whoever believes in him shall not perish but have eternal life.

* **Matthew 1:23** "The virgin will conceive and give birth to a son, and they will call him Immanuel" (which means "God with us").

* **Isaiah 53:4-5** ⁴Surely he took up our pain and bore our suffering, yet we considered him punished by God, stricken by him, and afflicted. ⁵But he was pierced for our transgressions, he was crushed for our iniquities; the punishment that brought us peace was on him, and by his wounds we are healed.

* **John 1:29** The next day John saw Jesus coming toward him and said, "Look, the Lamb of God, who takes away the sin of the world!

* **Romans 5:8** But God demonstrates his own love for us in this: While we were still sinners, Christ died for us.

* **John 14:6** Jesus answered, "I am the way and the truth and the life. No one comes to the Father except through me.

What happened to Jesus after that?

* **1 Corinthians 15:3-5** ³For what I received I passed on to you as of first importance: that Christ died for our sins according to the Scriptures, ⁴that he was buried, that he was raised on the third day according to the Scriptures, ⁵and that he appeared to Cephas, and then to the Twelve.

* **Acts 1:3** After his suffering, he presented himself to them and gave many convincing proofs that he was alive. He appeared to them over a period of forty days and spoke about the kingdom of God.

* **Hebrews 10:12** But when this priest had offered for all time one sacrifice for sins, he sat down at the right hand of God,

* **Psalm 110:5** The Lord is at your right hand; he will crush kings on the day of his wrath.

* **2 Thessalonians 1:7-8** ⁷and give relief to you who are troubled, and to us as well. This will happen when the Lord Jesus is revealed from heaven in blazing fire with his powerful angels. ⁸He will punish those who do not know God and do not obey the gospel of our Lord Jesus.

* **2 Timothy 4:1** In the presence of God and of Christ Jesus, who will judge the living and the dead, and in view of his appearing and his kingdom, I give you this charge:

* **2 Peter 3:9-12** ⁹The Lord is not slow in keeping his promise, as some understand slowness. Instead he is patient with you, not wanting anyone to perish, but everyone to come to repentance. ¹⁰But the day of the Lord will come like a thief. The heavens will disappear with a roar; the elements will be destroyed by fire, and the earth and everything done in it will be laid bare. ¹¹Since everything will be destroyed in this way, what kind of people ought you to be? You ought to live holy and godly lives ¹²as you look forward to the day of God and speed its coming. That day will bring about the destruction of the heavens by fire, and the elements will melt in the heat.

13 Then, what should I do?

* **1 John 3:1** See what great love the Father has lavished on us, that we should be called children of God! And that is what we are! The reason the world does not know us is that it did not know him.

* **Galatians 3:26** So in Christ Jesus you are all children of God through faith,

* **Romans 10:10** For it is with your heart that you believe and are justified, and it is with your mouth that you profess your faith and are saved.

* **Matthew 10:32** "Whoever acknowledges me before others, I will also acknowledge before my Father in heaven.

* **John 15:5-6** [5]"I am the vine; you are the branches. If you remain in me and I in you, you will bear much fruit; apart from me you can do nothing, [6]"If you do not remain in me, you are like a branch that is thrown away and withers; such branches are picked up, thrown into the fire and burned.

* **John 5:24** "Very truly I tell you, whoever hears my word and believes him who sent me has eternal life and will not be judged but has crossed over from death to life.

* **John 14:6** Jesus answered, "I am the way and the truth and the life. No one comes to the Father except through me.

* **Revelation 3:20** Here I am! I stand at the door and knock. If anyone hears my voice and opens the door, I will come in and eat with that person, and they with me. (Similar verse: **Luke 12:36**)

14 The Salvation Prayer

* **John 3:16** For God so loved the world that he gave his one and only Son, that whoever believes in him shall not perish but have eternal life.

* **Ephesians 2:8-9** ^{8}For it is by grace you have been saved, through faith — and this is not from yourselves, it is the gift of God — ^{9}not by works, so that no one can boast.

* **John 1:12** Yet to all who did receive him, to those who believed in his name, he gave the right to become children of God —

* **John 14:6** Jesus answered, "I am the way and the truth and the life. No one comes to the Father except through me.

* **Acts 4:12** Salvation is found in no one else, for there is no other name under heaven given to mankind by which we must be saved."

15 Then, what should I do from now on?

* **John 3:36** Whoever believes in the Son has eternal life, but whoever rejects the Son will not see life, for God's wrath remains on them.

* **1 Corinthians 15:22** For as in Adam all die, so in Christ all will be made alive.

* **1 John 5:13** I write these things to you who believe in the name of the Son of God so that you may know that you have eternal life.

* **1 Peter 5:8** Be alert and of sober mind. Your enemy the devil prowls around like a roaring lion looking for someone to devour.

* **Matthew 13:19-23** [19]When anyone hears the message about the kingdom and does not understand it, the evil one comes and snatches away what was sown in their heart. This is the seed sown along the path. [20]The seed falling on rocky ground refers to someone who hears the word and at once receives it with joy. [21]But since they have no root, they last only a short time. When trouble or persecution comes because of the word, they quickly fall away. [22]The seed falling among the thorns refers to someone who hears the word, but the worries of this life and the deceitfulness of wealth choke the word, making it unfruitful. [23]But the seed falling on good soil refers to someone who hears the word and understands it. This is the one who produces a crop, yielding a hundred, sixty or thirty times what was sown."

* **Ecclesiastes 4:9-12** [9]Two are better than one, because they have a good return for their labor: [10]If either of them falls down, one can help the other up. But pity anyone who falls and has no one to help them up. [11]Also, if two lie down together, they will keep warm. But how can one keep warm alone? [12]Though one may be overpowered, two can defend themselves. A cord of three strands is not quickly broken.

* **Hebrews 3:13** But encourage one another daily, as long as it is called "Today," so that none of you may be hardened by sin's deceitfulness.

* **Joshua 1:8** Keep the Book of the Law always on your lips: meditate on it day and night, so that you may be careful to do everything written in it.

* **1 John 2:5** But if anyone obeys his word, love for God is truly made complete in them. This is how we know we are in him.

* **Matthew 18:19-20** ¹⁹"Again, truly I tell you that if two of you on earth agree about anything they ask for, it will be done for them by my Father in heaven. ²⁰For where two or three gather in my name, there am I with them."

* **1 Thessalonians 5:16-18** ¹⁶Rejoice always, ¹⁷pray continually, ¹⁸give thanks in all circumstances; for this is God's will for you in Christ Jesus.

* **John 13:34-35** ³⁴"A new command I give you: Love one another. As I have loved you, so you must love one another. ³⁵By this everyone will know that you are my disciples, if you love one another."

16 Where should we go?

* **Ephesians 1:22-23** ²²And God placed all things under his feet and appointed him to be head over everything for the church, ²³which is his body, the fullness of him who fills everything in every way.

* **Romans 10:17** Consequently, faith comes from hearing the message, and the message is heard through the word about Christ.

* **John 16:13** But when he, the Spirit of truth, comes, he will guide you into all the truth. He will not speak on his own; he will speak only what he hears, and he will tell you what is yet to come.

* **Jeremiah 33:3** 'Call to me and I will answer you and tell you great and unsearchable things you do not know.'

* **Psalm 120:1** I call on the LORD in my distress, and he answers me.

* **Hebrews 13:15** Through Jesus, therefore, let us continually offer to God a sacrifice of praise — the fruit of lips that openly profess his name.

* **Ephesians 6:10-11, 18** [10]Finally, be strong in the Lord and in his mighty power. [11]Put on the full armor of God, so that you can take your stand against the devil's schemes. [18]And pray in the Spirit on all occasions with all kinds of prayers and requests. With this in mind, be alert and always keep on praying for all the Lord's people.

* **Acts 2:42, 46-47** [42]They devoted themselves to the apostles' teaching and to fellowship, to the breaking of bread and to prayer. [46]Every day they continued to meet together in the temple courts. They broke bread in their homes and ate together with glad and sincere hearts, [47]praising God and enjoying the favor of all the people. And the Lord added to their number daily those who were being saved.